Ugh! Yuck! and Whoa!

Back Off, Buddy!

World Book, Inc.
180 North LaSalle Street
Suite 900
Chicago, Illinois 60601
USA

For information about other World Book publications, visit our website at **www.worldbook.com** or call **1-800-WORLDBK (967-5325)**.

Library of Congress Cataloging-in-Publication data has been applied for.
Title: Ugh! Yuck! and Whoa! Back Off, Buddy!
ISBN: 978-0-7166-3709-7

Ugh! Yuck! and Whoa!
ISBN: 978-0-7166-3708-0 (set, hc)

Also available as:
ISBN: 978-0-7166-3717-2 (e-book)

1st printing July 2018

STAFF

Executive Committee

President
Jim O'Rourke

Vice President and Editor in Chief
Paul A. Kobasa

Vice President, Finance
Donald D. Keller

Vice President, Marketing
Jean Lin

Vice President, International
Maksim Rutenberg

Vice President, Technology
Jason Dole

Director, Human Resources
Bev Ecker

Editorial

Director, Print Publishing
Tom Evans

Writer
Grace Guibert

Editor
Will Adams

Manager, Contracts & Compliance (Rights & Permissions)
Loranne K. Shields

Manager, Indexing Services
David Pofelski

Librarian
S. Thomas Richardson

Digital

Director, Digital Product Development
Erika Meller

Digital Product Manager
Jonathan Wills

Manufacturing/ Production

Manufacturing Manager
Anne Fritzinger

Proofreader
Nathalie Strassheim

Graphics and Design

Senior Art Director
Tom Evans

Senior Designer
Don Di Sante

Media Editor
Rosalia Bledsoe

Special thanks to:

Nature Picture Library

Introduction

Nature is filled with some amazing creatures. From ocean bottoms to mountain tops, from hot deserts to freezing tundra, the *Ugh! Yuck! and Whoa!* books highlight the most extreme animals: the grossest, the deadliest, the strangest, and the ugliest! This book is all about animal **defenses. Defenses** are the ways in which animals protect themselves from harm. Animals use all sorts of **defenses** to stay safe from **predators** (animals that hunt, catch, and eat other animals). Some bite, some spray, some hide, and some sting. The animals that **predators** hunt and eat are called their **prey.** Read on to learn about some of the coolest and craziest ways that animals stay safe when they are threatened! This Defense Strength meter will show each animal's defensive power.

DEFENSE METER

MEDIUM

BRAZILIAN THREE-BANDED ARMADILLO

The Brazilian three-banded armadillo can curl up into a tight ball to defend itself.

Armadillos are mammals protected by a shell made up of small, bony pieces. The shell covers their back. Three narrow strips, or bands, in the middle of the shell work like hinges. The hinges allow the armadillo to bend its shell and curl up.

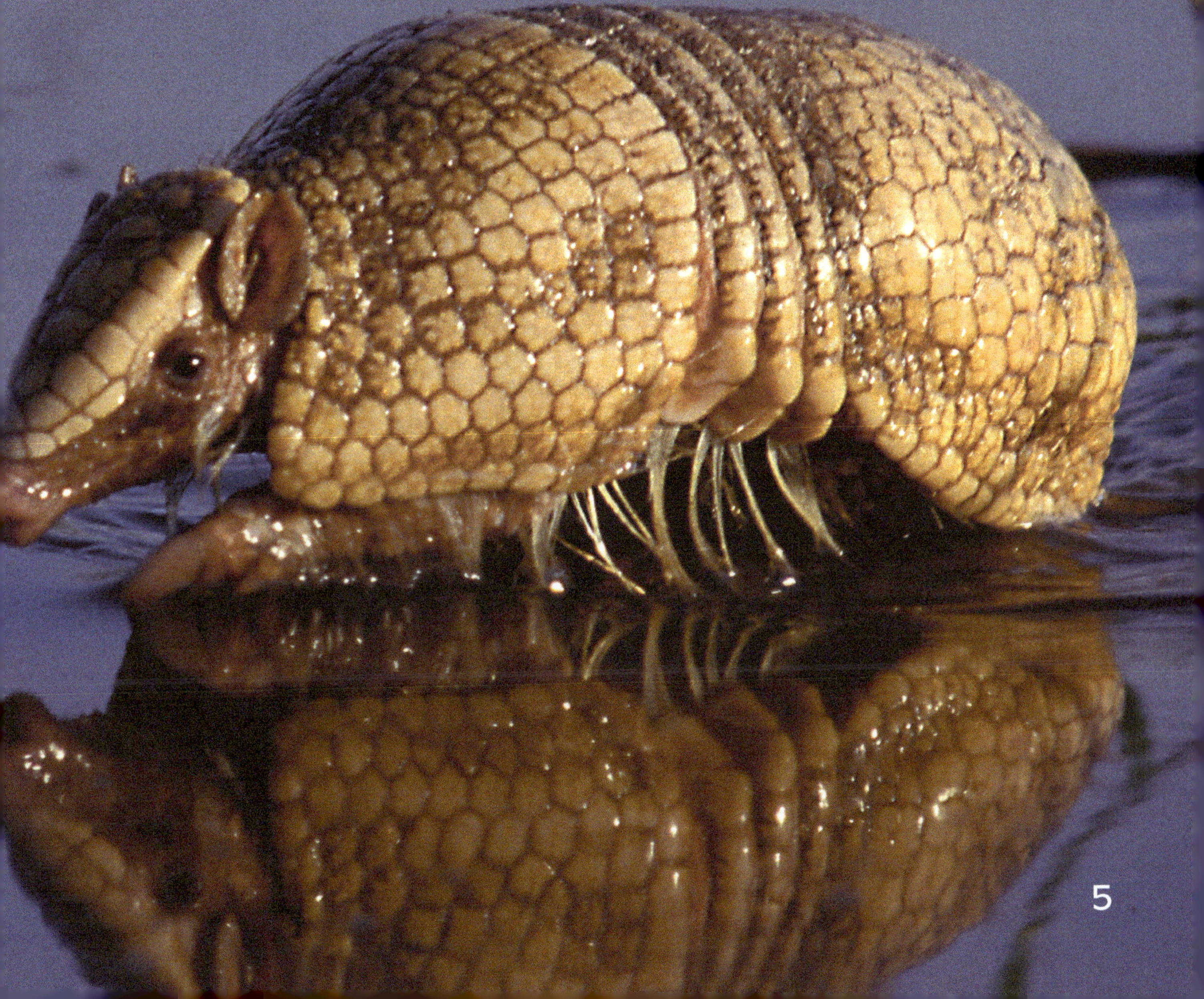

More Armored Animals

These animals also use their hard outer shells like armor. When they ball up, their armor keeps them safe from **predators!**

Pill bugs

Cuckoo wasp

Armadillo lizard

Pangolin

PORCUPINEFISH

A porcupinefish, sometimes called a *puffer fish* or *blowfish,* is a type of fish with pointy spines covering its body. When an enemy scares a porcupinefish, the fish can fill its stomach with water. The fish blows up like a balloon and its spines stick straight out, ready to give a predator a painful prick!

POISON DART FROG

Poison dart frogs are small, colorful frogs with poisonous skin! The poison on the frogs' skin helps protect them from being eaten. There are more than 200 types of poison dart frog. Native people in the South American country of Colombia used poison from these frogs on darts for hunting. This gave the poison dart frog its name.

The poison on the skin of the golden poison dart frog is strong enough to kill 20,000 mice or 10 people with less than one drop! This frog grows to be about the same length and weight as an average paper clip. Golden poison dart frogs are 1 inch (25 millimeters) long.

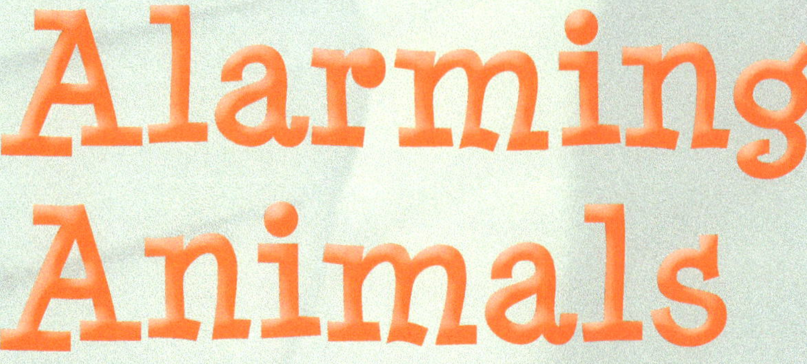

Alarming Animals

Some animals use colors and patterns to keep **predators** away. Colors like red, yellow, and black and patterns like bold stripes mean danger!

Skunk

Coral snake

Bumble bee

Flamboyant cuttlefish

(flam BOY uhnt means showy)

Poison dart frogs

FIRE-BELLIED TOAD

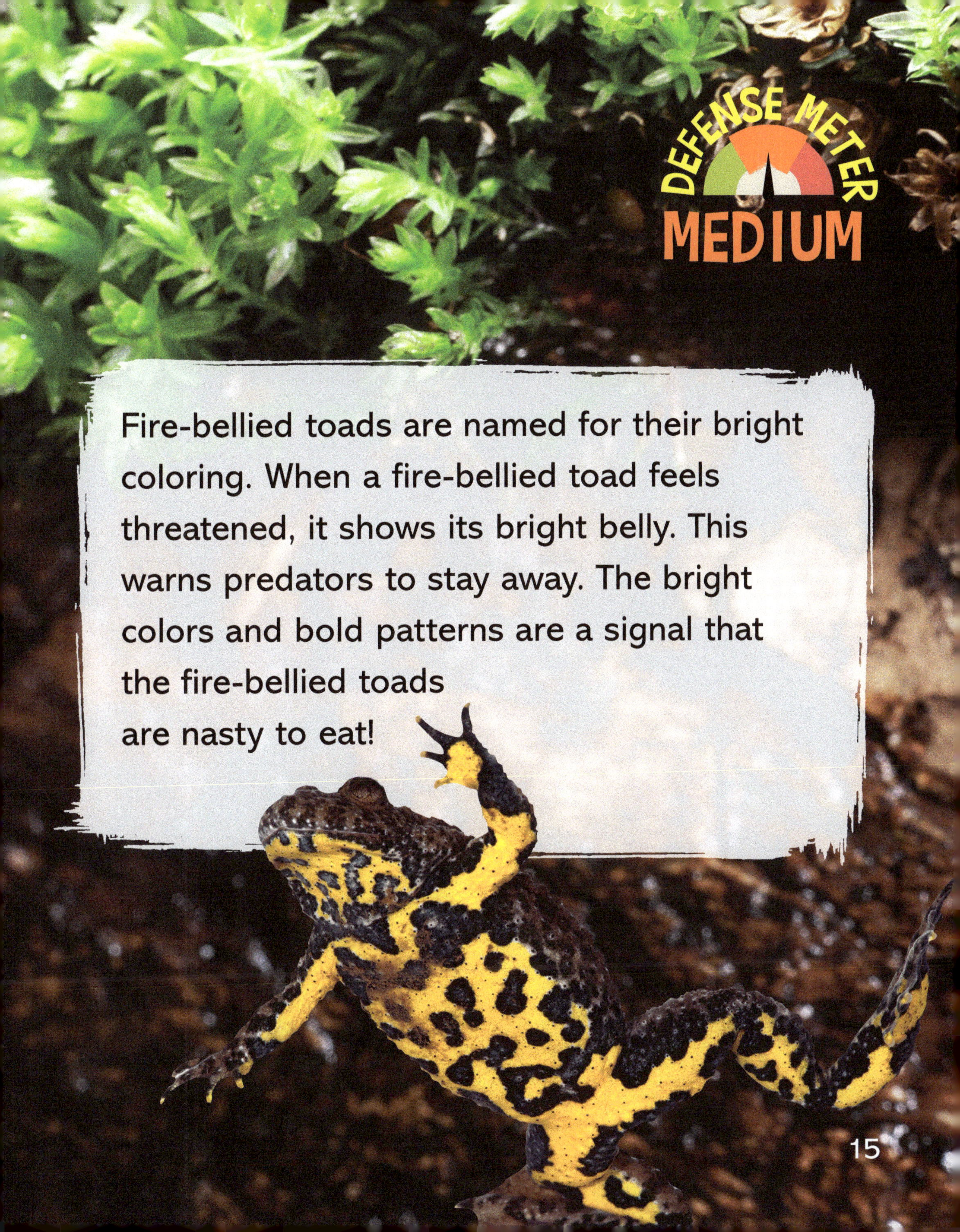

Fire-bellied toads are named for their bright coloring. When a fire-bellied toad feels threatened, it shows its bright belly. This warns predators to stay away. The bright colors and bold patterns are a signal that the fire-bellied toads are nasty to eat!

BLUE-RINGED OCTOPUS

They are small, but blue-ringed octopuses are among the deadliest animals in the ocean. They use **venom** to hunt crabs, shrimp, and fish. But if a human touches a blue-ringed octopus, it can be deadly. The **venom** in one blue-ringed octopus could kill 26 adult humans in minutes. The **venom** has not one, but two deadly toxins, or poisons!

DEFENSE METER
HIGH

LIONFISH

Lionfish have **venomous** spines. The spines protect lionfish from predators. Stings can be deadly to other fish—and very painful for people! The spines and fins resemble a lion's mane, giving lionfish their name.

PORCUPINE

Yuck!

Some quills have sharp ends that point backwards. They are called **barbs. Barbs** make quills stick in the porcupine's enemies! **Barbed** quills hurt and are hard to get out.

Porcupines are mammals that have strong, stiff quills on their back, sides, and tail. Quills are long, sharp groups of hairs that grow together. Porcupines raise and shake their quills to warn enemies. If they are attacked, porcupines stick their sharp quills into **predators.**

ZORILLA

The zorilla, also called the striped polecat, is like a skunk. It is protective of its territory. If a zorilla feels threatened, it will spray a nasty smelling liquid at its enemy! A zorilla's spray is stronger and smellier than a skunk's. The liquid is so strong that it can blind the zorilla's attacker!

BOMBARDIER BEETLE

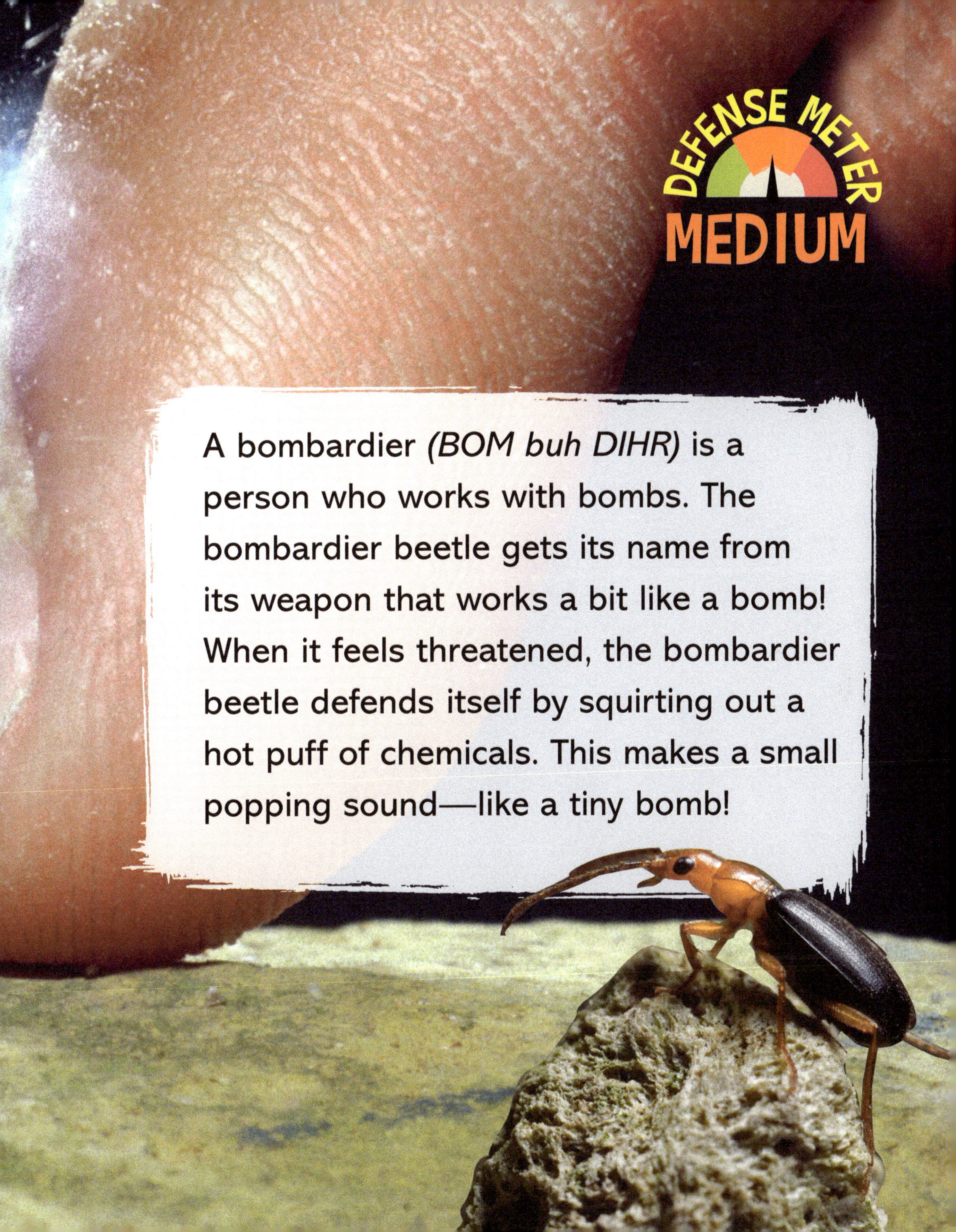

A bombardier *(BOM buh DIHR)* is a person who works with bombs. The bombardier beetle gets its name from its weapon that works a bit like a bomb! When it feels threatened, the bombardier beetle defends itself by squirting out a hot puff of chemicals. This makes a small popping sound—like a tiny bomb!

HORNET

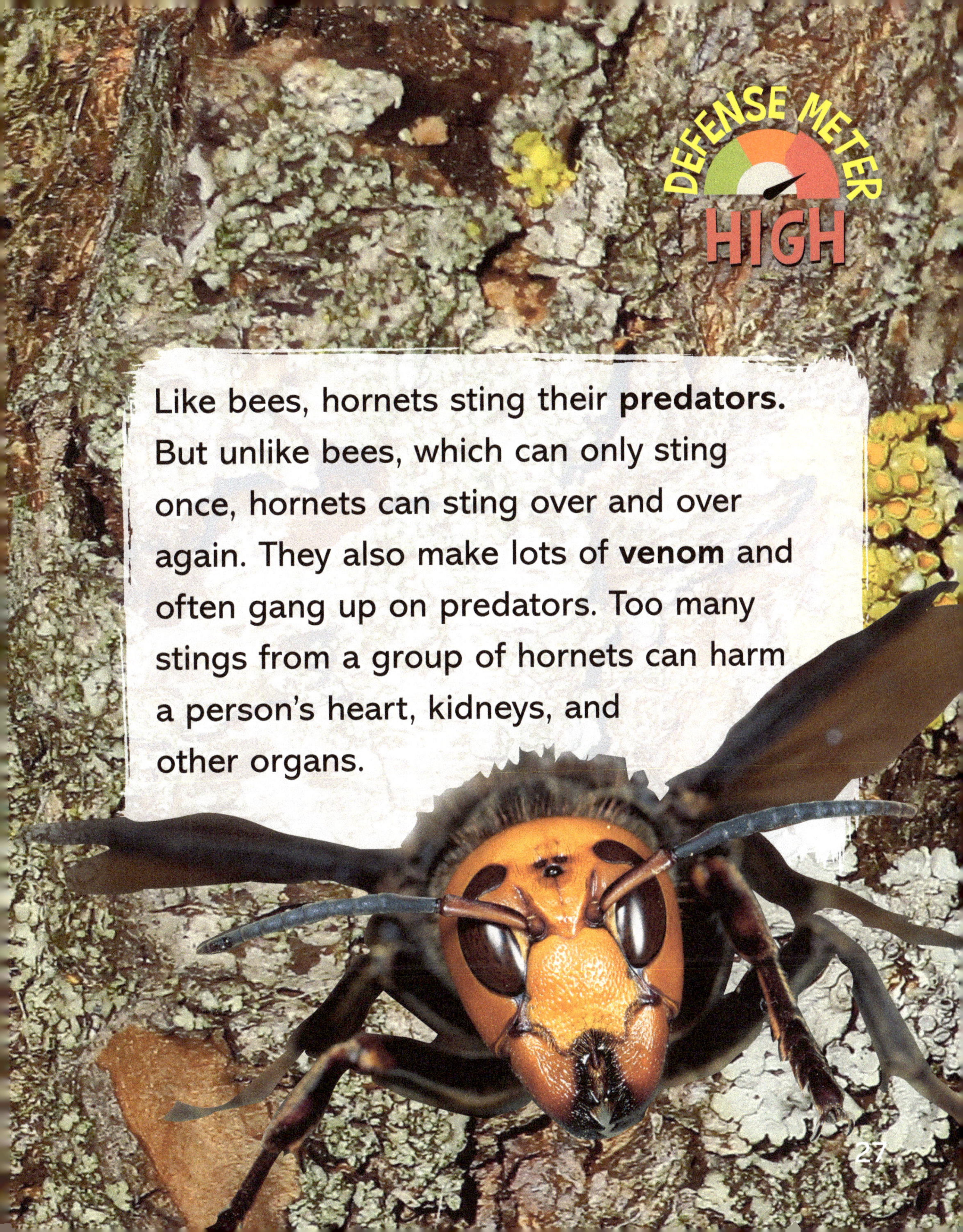

Like bees, hornets sting their **predators.** But unlike bees, which can only sting once, hornets can sting over and over again. They also make lots of **venom** and often gang up on predators. Too many stings from a group of hornets can harm a person's heart, kidneys, and other organs.

TEXAS HORNED LIZARD

The Texas horned lizard is built for **defense.** It is covered in prickly spines. Its coloring helps it blend into the sand and rock where it lives. If a **predator** catches the Texas horned lizard, it puffs up its body, making it hard to swallow whole.

DEFENSE METER
LOW

Yuck!

If some kinds of predators, such as cats and coyotes, catch a Texas horned lizard, it shoots blood from the corners of its eyes into the predator's mouth! The blood tastes bad to these predators, so they let the lizard go. The lizard can shoot its blood as far as 5 feet (1.5 meters) away!

SPANISH RIBBED NEWT

Newts are a type of **amphibian.** Like most **amphibians,** newts spend part of their time living on land and part of their time in the water. The Spanish ribbed newt uses its ribs (bones in the chest) as weapons! It can push its ribs outside of its skin to poke its predators. The Spanish ribbed newt also has a special toxin (poison) that it uses to sting predators.

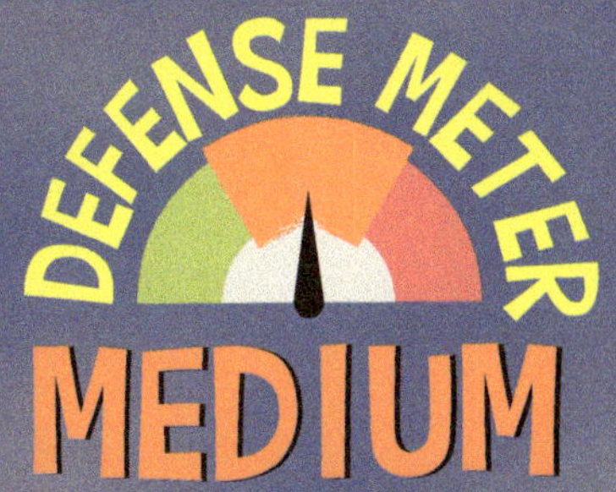

FRILLED LIZARD

When it feels threatened, the frilled lizard puts on a flashy show. It extends a wide flap of skin around its neck to make it appear larger. The frills can reach 1 foot (0.3 meters) across and come in bright colors like red, orange, green, or black. The frilled lizard stands on its back legs and hisses to scare off its predators!

TERMITES

Different termites play different parts in their **colony.** Most are workers that take care of the nest. When the workers of some kinds of termites get old, they grow into a special **defense** for the **colony:** they can explode! These termites give their lives to protect the others in their **colony** from predators.

DEFENSE METER
MEDIUM

GRASS SNAKES

Grass snakes are not the only animals to play dead. Opossums have a similar reaction when they face danger!

Some snakes have **venomous** bites to protect themselves from **predators.** Grass snakes, a type of snake that lives near water, are not **venomous.** To keep **predators** away, grass snakes sometimes play dead! Many **predators** will not eat animals that are—or seem to be—dead. Picky eaters!

LIZARD

Many lizards have long tails. If a **predator** catches a lizard by the tail, the tail can break off, and the lizard can get away!

DEFENSE METER
LOW
Some lizards can grow a new tail after losing the old one!
Ugh!

SQUID

Squids have many ways to avoid their **predators.** Some squids can change color! They can blend in with their surroundings, helping them hide from **predators.**

Whoa!

All squids have an ink sac that squirts out a dark fluid when the squid swims away from danger. The fluid hides the squid as it escapes!

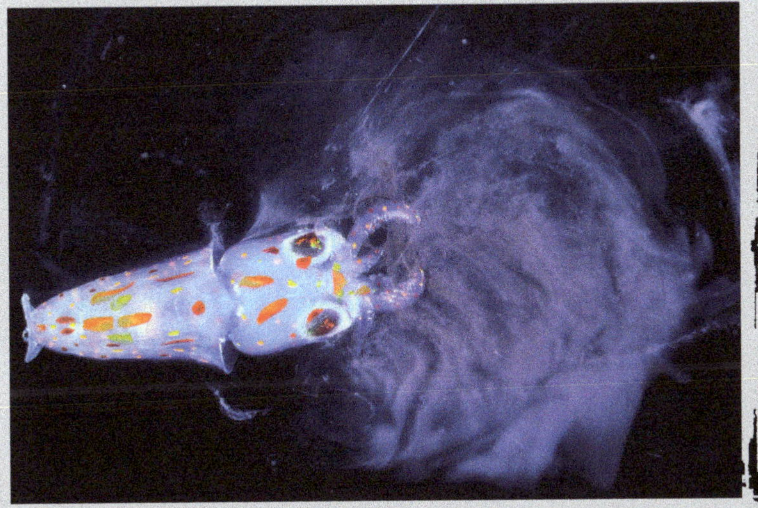

FULMAR

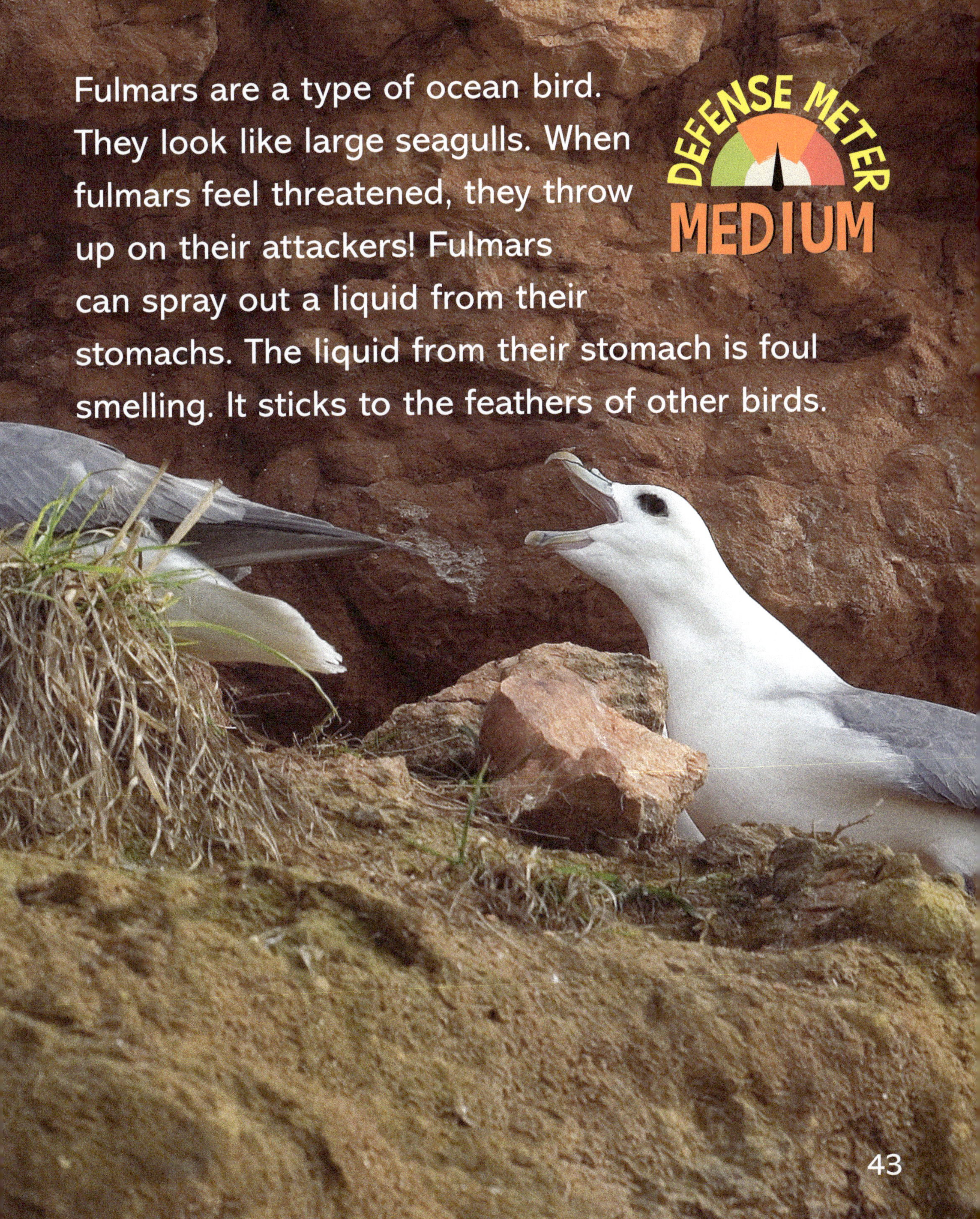

Fulmars are a type of ocean bird. They look like large seagulls. When fulmars feel threatened, they throw up on their attackers! Fulmars can spray out a liquid from their stomachs. The liquid from their stomach is foul smelling. It sticks to the feathers of other birds.

ELECTRIC EEL

Whoa!

Electric eels are not the only electric animals. Some kinds of a group of fish called rays can also give strong electric shocks!

DEFENSE METER

LOW

The electric eel is a long, narrow fish. It can give off a strong electric shock—up to 650 volts! That's about six times the voltage of a household power outlet—powerful enough to kill other fish. It can even stun a human being. The electric eel uses its shock to kill its **prey** and to escape from its **predators.**

Glossary

Amphibian

one of a group of cold-blooded animals with a backbone and moist, smooth skin, such as frogs and salamanders.

Barb

a sharp point that sticks out backward.

Colony

a group of living things of one kind that live together or grow in the same place.

Defense

the act of guarding or protecting.

Predator

an animal that hunts, kills, and eats other animals.

Prey

an animal that is hunted, killed, and eaten by another; to hunt, kill, and eat another animal.

Venom

a liquid that an animal makes to stun, injure, or kill another animal through biting or stinging.

Venomous

poisonous; producer of venom

Index

Acknowledgments

Cover: © Nick Garbutt, Nature Picture Library; © David Fleetham, Nature Picture Library

4-5 © Luiz Claudio Marigo, Nature Picture Library; © Mark Payne-Gill, Nature Picture Library

6-7 © Stephen Dalton, Nature Picture Library; © Marc Pihet, MYN/ Nature Picture Library; © InsectWorld/Shutterstock; © Miles Barton, Nature Picture Library; © Roland Seitre, Nature Picture Library; © Mike Wilkes, Nature Picture Library

8-9 © Claudio Contreras, Nature Picture Library; © David Fleetham, Nature Picture Library

10-11 © Nick Garbutt, Nature Picture Library; © Edwin Giesbers, Nature Picture Library; © AVS-Images/Shutterstock

12-13 © Alex Hyde, Nature Picture Library; © Rolf Nussbaumer, Nature Picture Library; © Seth Patterson, MYN/Nature Picture Library; © Clay Bolt, MLN/Nature Picture Library; © Tim Laman, Nature Picture Library

14-15 © Adrian Davies, Nature Picture Library; © Dirk Funhoff, MLN/ Nature Picture Library

16-17 © Teguh Tirtaputra, Shutterstock

18-19 © David Fleetham, Nature Picture Library

20-21 © Klein & Hubert, Nature Picture Library; © John Cancalosi, Nature Picture Library

22-23 © Martin Harvey, Alamy Images

24-25 © Nature Production/Nature Picture Library; © Stephen Dalton, Nature Picture Library

26-27 © Xpixel/Shutterstock; © Nature Production/Nature Picture Library

28-29 © Rolf Nussbaumer, Nature Picture Library; © AP Photo

30-31 © Klein & Hubert, Nature Picture Library

32-33 © Dave Watts, Nature Picture Library

34-35 © Khlung Center/Shutterstock

36-37 © Daniel Heuclin, Nature Picture Library; © Phil Savoie, Nature Picture Library

38-39 © Nature Production/Nature Picture Library; © Fabio Liverani, Nature Picture Library

40-41 © Reinhard Dirscherl, ullstein bild/Getty Images; © Nature Production/Nature Picture Library

42-43 © Ernie Janes, Nature Picture Library; © Simon Wagen, J Downer Product/Nature Picture Library

44-45 © Vladimir Wrangel, Shutterstock; © Sue Daly, Nature Picture Library

www.ingramcontent.com/pod-product-compliance
Ingram Content Group UK Ltd.
Pitfield, Milton Keynes, MK11 3LW, UK
UKHW061956290726
14090UKWH00021B/1249

9 780716 650829